Reflecting on Growth at University and College

A Workbook for Final-Year Students

Adam Morgan

Sydney, Australia

Copyright © 2025 Adam Morgan

All rights reserved. Except to the extent permitted by law, no part of this publication may be reproduced, distributed, or transmitted in any form or by any means, including photocopying, recording, or other electronic or mechanical methods, without the prior written permission of the author. The author can be contacted via adam-morgan.com.au.

The information contained in this workbook is for educational purposes. No warranties of any kind are declared or implied. By engaging with this workbook, the user agrees that under no circumstances is the author responsible for any damages or losses, direct or indirect, that are incurred as a result of the use of the information contained within this workbook, including, but not limited to, errors, omissions, or inaccuracies.

ISBN 978-0-6456794-6-5

Published by Adam Morgan

Design and Layout:
Ilka Staudinger-Morgan

Contents

Introduction		1
Part A	**Considering Growth**	**3**
	1. Knowledge and Learning	4
	2. Higher-Order Thinking	6
	3. Written Communication	8
	4. Verbal Communication	10
	5. Teamwork	12
	6. Self-Management	14
	7. Problem-Solving	16
	8. Global Citizenship	18
	9. A Growth Area of Your Choice	20
Part B	**Reconsidering Growth**	**23**
	10. Biggest Growth Areas	24
	11. Future Growth Areas	26
	12. Next Steps and Using Growth	28
	13. Expressing Growth	30
Conclusion		33
References		34

Introduction

This workbook will help you look at your growth during your time as a student. Your institution wanted you to grow in many areas during your studies and created a rich environment to help this happen. Throughout these pages, you will reflect on some of these growth areas.

Completing this workbook is straightforward. First, you will be asked to consider your growth in several important areas. Later, you will be asked to reconsider what you have written so you can draw more meaning from your entries.

When you have completed this workbook, you will have captured many important insights about yourself and your growth. You will have identified your biggest growth areas, your future growth areas, and how your growth will be applied as you take your next professional steps. You will also have the words needed to describe yourself and your growth when required in the future (e.g., in an interview).

This workbook requires you to write entries. In terms of the amount you write and the quality of your entries, this depends on how you have come about engaging with this workbook. If you are completing this workbook as part of your personal development, with no institutional expectations or requirements, then the amount you write and the quality of your entries is your decision to make. You can write as little or as much as you like in the spaces provided, and the quality of your entries is also up to you. If the completion of this workbook is a requirement at your institution, however, it is important that you clarify what is expected of you. There might be specific expectations regarding the amount you have to write and the quality of your entries.

The ability to write entries in this workbook will vary. Some will find it easy; others might find it more challenging. If you are stuck or looking for suggestions, some 'you might like to consider' prompts are given. They are just suggestions to help if needed. You do not need to address every prompt given. You should also try verbalizing your responses before trying to write them down. Finally, you should consider drafting your responses elsewhere before transferring them to this workbook.

Part A

Considering Growth

In this first part of the workbook, several knowledge and skill areas are presented. Your task is to write entries about these areas based on your experiences. There are nine areas covered in this first part. These are:

- Knowledge and Learning
- Higher-Order Thinking
- Written Communication
- Verbal Communication
- Teamwork
- Self-Management
- Problem-Solving
- Global Citizenship
- A Growth Area of Your Choice

1. Knowledge and Learning

Universities and colleges are places where passionate experts create and disseminate knowledge. Your teachers/instructors and support staff curated the knowledge you engaged with. They carefully considered what you should be learning and designed innovative ways to help you acquire this knowledge. You have no doubt benefited from their efforts and have become a more knowledgeable person as a result.

In the space provided on the next page, write about your growth related to knowledge and learning. You might like to consider:

- What you now know compared to when you started your studies.
- How your growth in this area came about (e.g., through particular assignments, readings, teaching methods, peer interactions, specific courses or workshops).
- The challenges you might have faced in learning and how you overcame them.
- Some areas where you feel particularly knowledgeable.

My growth related to knowledge and learning:

2. Higher-Order Thinking

Universities and colleges are higher education institutions. You were introduced to complex theories, concepts, and ideas. You were required to make sense of them, critically evaluate them, apply them in new ways, consider their limitations, and extend their utility, to name a few. You made judgments on your work and that produced by other students. You also defended your opinions and ideas. All these actions involve complex, higher-order thinking. You have been constantly required to think in higher-order ways and have thus grown in this area.

In the space provided on the next page, write about your growth related to higher-order thinking. You might like to consider:

- How you now think compared to when you started your studies.
- How your growth in this area came about (e.g., through particular assignments, class discussions, debates, peer interactions, specific courses or workshops).
- The challenges you might have faced in relation to higher-order thinking and how you overcame them.
- Some of your higher-order thinking strengths (e.g., thinking critically, making sense of complex matters, seeing connections).

My growth related to higher-order thinking:

3. Written Communication

Communicating in the written form has been a central part of your studies. Essays, reports, sections in group reports, short and long answer responses in exams, blog posts, news articles, and presentation slides were some of the ways you might have written during your studies. Your writing was often assessed, with feedback given to help you improve. You might also have received feedback from family members, friends, peers, professionals in support roles, and online tools. Your institution might also have had specific initiatives to help you develop in this area (e.g., writing workshops, courses, drop-in sessions). All this writing and support has given you the opportunity to grow in this area.

In the space provided on the next page, write about your growth related to written communication. You might like to consider:

- How you now write compared to when you started your studies.
- How your growth in this area came about (e.g., through particular assignments, receiving feedback, specific classes, courses or workshops).
- The challenges you might have faced in becoming a better writer and how you overcame them.
- Some of your written communication strengths (e.g., writing essays, writing concisely, writing for social media, writing critically).

My growth related to written communication:

4. Verbal Communication

Your student experience also involved communicating verbally. You would have participated in many verbal-based activities during your studies, such as class discussions, debates, role-plays, and group work. You might also have made class presentations or similar performances (e.g., demonstrations, pitches). There was also a lot of informal verbal communication during your studies, such as speaking with other students, staff members, and people in the broader community. Your institution might also have had specific initiatives to help you develop in this area (e.g., workshops, courses, sessions). You had the potential to grow as a verbal communicator during your studies.

In the space provided on the next page, write about your growth related to verbal communication. You might like to consider:

- How you now speak compared to when you started your studies.
- How your growth in this area came about (e.g., through particular assignments, class discussions, peer interactions, specific classes, courses or workshops).
- The challenges you might have faced in becoming a better speaker and how you overcame them.
- Some of your strengths as a verbal communicator (e.g., making formal presentations, projecting your voice, modulating your pitch, making 'small talk').

My growth related to verbal communication:

5. Teamwork

Your educational institution has given you the opportunity to work with others in groups throughout your studies. You would have participated in group assignments/projects and class discussion groups. You might have been part of a study group, a sports team, a social club, or a student committee. You also made new friends and acquaintances during your studies and did things together with them in groups. By working in groups, you had the opportunity to develop your teamwork skills, such as:*

- Listening actively
- Communicating constructively
- Helping
- Leading
- Following the lead of others
- Treating others with respect
- Responding to conflict
- Motivating others
- Contributing to group meetings
- Working as a problem-solver
- Showing flexibility
- Demonstrating reliability
- Fostering constructive group climates

In the space provided on the next page, write about your growth related to teamwork. You might like to consider:

- How you now work in teams/groups compared to when you started your studies.
- How your growth in this area came about (e.g., through particular assignments, peer interactions, specific classes, courses or workshops).
- The challenges you might have faced in becoming a better team player and how you overcame them.
- Some of your strengths as a team player (e.g., from the areas listed above).

---

* Drawn from frameworks proposed by Brounstein (2002), Wheelan (2015), and the Association of American Colleges and Universities (AAC&U).

My growth related to teamwork:

6. Self-Management

There are many demands placed on university and college students. There is never enough time to do everything you need to do. There are classes to attend, class preparation to do, research to be undertaken, papers to write, online tasks to engage with, and group meetings to attend, to name a few. You must do all this along with the numerous other demands on your time, such as work commitments, family responsibilities, co-curricular/extra-curricular activities, appointments, maintaining friendships, and making time for yourself. How you went about managing these competing demands was your responsibility. You were expected to self-manage and have thus been given the opportunity to grow in this area.

In the space provided on the next page, write about your growth related to self-management. You might like to consider:

- How you now self-manage compared to when you started your studies.
- How your growth in this area came about (e.g., through trial and error, learning from others, reading a book, specific classes, courses or workshops).
- The challenges you might have faced with self-management and how you overcame them.
- Some of your self-management strengths (e.g., making 'to do' lists, setting up reminders, making a timetable, self-discipline).

My growth related to self-management:

7. Problem-Solving

Universities and colleges are complex places that work with complicated issues. Dealing with ill-defined and challenging problems is the norm. The teachers/instructors and support staff at your institution constantly operate with complexity. They research and teach complex topics. In higher education, they also expect their students to operate in this complex space. The topics you engaged with were very complex. The assignments you undertook were complex and challenging. The dynamics within your group assignments/projects might have been sometimes challenging. The management of your workload might also have been challenging at times. You were constantly solving problems. This was another opportunity for you to grow, this time as a problem-solver.

In the space provided on the next page, write about your growth related to problem-solving. You might like to consider:

- How you now solve problems compared to when you started your studies.
- How your growth in this area came about (e.g., through trial and error, learning from others, reading a book, specific classes, courses or workshops).
- The challenges you might have faced in becoming a better problem-solver and how you overcame them.
- Some of your problem-solving strengths (e.g., perspective-taking, experimenting, consulting others).

My growth related to problem-solving:

8. Global Citizenship

Universities and colleges have considerable diversity within them. The teaching and support staff at your institution are diverse. They come from different parts of the world or country. They have different upbringings, experiences, and world views. The students at your institution are equally diverse. You were fortunate to experience this diversity at a much closer level. You listened to them in class. You worked alongside them during in-class activities. You worked with them on group assignments/projects. They helped and supported you. You learned from them. You gained insights into how they think, solve problems, and communicate, to name a few. The topics you engaged with were also diverse. You were introduced to a vast array of theories and concepts. You have become more knowledgeable about local, national, and international affairs. You understand the modern world better and how one operates in diverse environments.

In the space provided on the next page, write about your growth related to global citizenship. You might like to consider:

- How you now view the world and its citizens compared to when you started your studies.
- How your growth in this area came about (e.g., through self-reflection, particular assignments, class discussions, peer interactions, specific classes, courses or workshops).
- The challenges you might have faced in becoming a global citizen and how you overcame them.
- Some of your strengths as a global citizen (e.g., working in diverse groups, perspective-taking, being open to new experiences).

My growth related to global citizenship:

9. A Growth Area of Your Choice

Up to this point, we have covered some of the main growth areas at university and college. There are, however, many others. Along with the ones covered thus far, your institution may have had additional growth areas, such as:

- Creativity
- Ethics
- Leadership
- Lifelong Learning
- Using Technology
- Entrepreneurship
- Quantitative Literacy
- Inquiry and Analysis
- Information Literacy
- Visual Communication

This is your chance to write about your growth in an area of your choosing. It can be one that is listed above or one not listed. It might be one specific to your institution's mission or one that you independently developed. It's your choice.

In the space provided on the next page, write about your growth in your chosen area. You might like to consider:

- How the growth in your chosen area came about (e.g., through self-reflection, particular assignments, class discussions, peer interactions, specific classes, courses or workshops).
- The challenges you might have faced in your chosen area and how you overcame them.
- Some of your strengths in your chosen area.

My growth related to _____

Part B

Reconsidering Growth

In Part A of this workbook, you wrote entries based on your perceived growth. In this second part, you will now reconsider these entries. This reconsidering is very important to do. It will help you make sense of your growth and see the bigger picture. Before we begin Part B, it is important that you re-read your entries. Once you have done this, there are four more short tasks to do. These are:

- Biggest Growth Areas
- Future Growth Areas
- Next Steps and Using Growth
- Expressing Growth

These tasks also have some 'you might like to consider' prompts to assist you. As in Part A, you do not need to address every prompt

10. Biggest Growth Areas

In the previous part of this workbook (Part A), you wrote entries related to your growth in various areas. In some of these areas, your growth might have been quite modest. In other areas, it was probably bigger. In these areas, you have been transformed in particular ways. You know and can do things that were not possible a few years ago, for example.

In the space provided on the next page, write about your biggest growth areas. You might like to consider:

- The areas where you grew the most.
- The areas where your growth has resulted in big improvements (e.g., your grades, opportunities).
- The areas where your growth had the biggest challenges to overcome.
- The areas that have had the biggest impact on your self-esteem.

You might also like to consider explaining:

- How you feel about this growth.
- What it means to you.

My biggest growth areas:

11. Future Growth Areas

In the previous task, you stated your biggest growth areas. However, this does not mean they cannot be further developed. Likewise, there are probably some areas that have not been developed enough during your studies. This might have been because you focused on some areas more than others. Alternatively, it might have been due to a lack of opportunity (e.g., it was not a focus at your institution). Either way, growth in these areas is important and should be a future focus of yours.

In the space provided on the next page, write about the growth areas you will target in the future. You might like to consider:

- Those areas where you would like to develop further.
- Those areas where you have had little opportunity to develop thus far (e.g., some of those listed on page 20).
- Those areas that you know might be needed in the future (e.g., in your future profession).

You might also like to consider how you will go about developing in your targeted areas. For example:

- Taking a short course.
- Reading a self-development book on the topic.
- Consulting others (e.g., a careers coach, friends, family members, a mentor, a staff member at your institution).

My future growth areas:

12. Next Steps and Using Growth

As a final-year/senior student, you are about to take your next steps. This might be further study. It might be employment. It might be a start-up venture or volunteering. Whatever it might be, your growth over the last few years will help you considerably. It will enable you to thrive in your next steps. You will be able to apply your growth. You will be able to help both yourself and others in the immediate future. Giving some targeted thought to this is important to do.

In the space provided on the next page, write about your next steps and some of the ways you will use your growth. You might like to consider:

- What your next steps will be.
- The abilities most required in your next steps.
- How your growth will help you.
- How your growth might help others in the immediate future.

My next steps and using my growth:

13. Expressing Growth

Throughout the pages of this workbook, you have captured many aspects of your growth and reconsidered them. It is now time to bring this all together onto one page.

This is the final task in this workbook, and it is a little different. Up to this point, all your entries have been written. In this task, you have the option to be more creative. All you need to do is express your growth on the opposite page. You can populate this page however you wish. You might like to populate it with keywords or phrases that capture your growth. Alternatively, you might like to draw something or make a collage. It is up to you. This is your chance to express your growth however you wish.

To do this task, you might like to consider:

- Your biggest growth areas.
- How you will apply your growth.
- The emotions evoked as you completed this workbook.
- The images, colors, and symbols reflected in your entries.

If you are struggling with ideas, you might like to consider entering the word 'growth' into your preferred search engine and seeing what images are shown. You might also do the same for other terms used in this workbook, such as knowledge, communication, higher-order thinking, teamwork, and problem-solving.

Note: There is no border on the opposite page. It has been left intentionally 'clean' so you can use the whole page, much like a blank canvas.

My growth:

Conclusion

This workbook has given you the opportunity to look at your growth during your time as a student. Each day you were a student at your institution, you were growing. You have just looked at some of this growth and written about it. Hopefully, you can see how much you have grown over the last few years and are proud of what you see.

Having completed this workbook, you should now be able to describe how you have grown during your studies. This should help you populate resumes, CVs, professional online profiles, and applications. You should also be better able to handle ability-related questions in interviews. Just remember to re-visit the pages of this workbook in preparation for such interviews. Hopefully, your efforts will be rewarded.

References

Association of American Colleges and Universities (AAC&U). *VALUE Rubrics - Teamwork*. Retrieved from https://www.aacu.org/initiatives/value-initiative/value-rubrics/value-rubrics-teamwork

Brounstein, M. (2002). *Managing teams for dummies.* New York: Wiley.

Wheelan, S. A. (2015). *Creating effective teams: A guide for members and leaders* (5th Ed.). Thousand Oaks, CA: Sage.

www.ingramcontent.com/pod-product-compliance
Lightning Source LLC
Chambersburg PA
CBHW051158290426
44109CB00022B/2510